Seven Giving

PRINCIPLES FOR BIBLICAL FINANCIAL SUCCESS

"7G"

BY. REV. GREG WRIGHT
MPPA, CPA

Certificate of Registration

This Certificate issued under the seal of the Copyright Office in accordance with title 17, *United States Code*, attests that registration has been made for the work identified below. The information on this certificate has been made a part of the Copyright Office records.

Shira Perlmutter

United States Register of Copyrights and Director

Registration Number

TXu 2-426-673

Effective Date of Registration:
April 22, 2024
Registration Decision Date:
April 29, 2024

Title

Title of Work: FINANCIAL STEWARDSHIP GUIDE

Previous or Alternate Title: 7G - Seven Giving Principles for Lifetime Financial Success

Completion/Publication

Year of Completion: 2013

Author

- **Author:** Gregory Gerard Wright
  Author Created: text, budget worksheet forms
  Citizen of: United States
  Year Born: 1957

Copyright Claimant

Copyright Claimant: Gregory Gerard Wright
511 Shingletown Rd, Mountain City, TN, 37683, United States

Certification

Name: Reginald Bruner
Date: April 19, 2024
Applicant's Tracking Number: 81168889

Correspondence: Yes
Copyright Office notes: Regarding authorship information: Deposit contains text.

7 GIVING PRINCIPLES

1. Attitude

Our attitude towards money. 1 Timothy 6:10

2. Priorities

Your priorities prepare the way. Matthew 6:33

3. Diligence

Diligence can be "tough stuff". Jeremiah 32:19

4. Accountability

Stewardship is most closely related to the idea of accountability. 1 Corinthians 4:2

5. Faith

Faith is a spiritual principle that functions in a world of substance and evidence. Hebrews 11:1

6. Generosity

Generosity must come from the heart, not a religious formula. Acts 20:35

7. Joy

Joy is an exhilarating human emotion that transcends happiness. 1 Chronicles 29:9

Vision

"Beloved, I pray that you may prosper in all things and be in health, just as your soul prospers." (3 John 1:2, NIV). "The reward of humility and the fear of the Lord are riches, honor, and life." (Proverbs 22:4, NIV)

God's word answers life's questions - the study of money holds no exception! An honest and diligent application of these seven Godly principles to your personal finances will calm any financial storm, plan for your future, and take you to a higher level of joyful giving.

This guidebook is intended to spark a financial revolution producing plenty in an era of debt, lack and poverty. "7" is a perfect number in the Holy Scriptures, and givers who are perfectly disposed towards the will and purpose of God can (and will) reach that perfect level of giving and abundance, 7G. (Lk. 6:38)

Experience the faithfulness of God's promises, the rewards of obedient financial stewardship, and the great joy of giving from abundance. In this practical and biblically principled guidebook are ancient and proven steps for a new generation of financial stewardship.

TABLE OF CONTENTS

Vision

Introduction

Chapters (7G Principles)

1. Attitude

2. Priorities

3. Diligence

4. Accountability

5. Faith

6. Generosity

7. Joy

Reference Notes

INTRODUCTION

One of America's wisest forefathers, Benjamin Franklin, discovered a key insight about money - a subject we often find difficult to understand and discuss, especially in church. Franklin understood that money can create money - that's right, it has a *prolific* nature. As Christ's followers, we must understand the basic truths about money and wealth so that we can be faithful stewards of the resources that God has entrusted to us. King Solomon recognized the prolific nature of money and therefore said, "The rich rule over the poor, and the borrower is servant to the lender" (Prov.22:7).

This course, Seven Giving Principles for Biblical Financial Success, 7G, is intended as a common-sense guide, written in understandable language, to help all believers handle wisely the resources entrusted to them. The book is intentionally written at a high level and can be further used to develop your own customized bible studies or personal devotions.

The Bible contains God's instructions for creating and managing wealth, and although many Americans may not consider themselves wealthy, we live in a very rich society when compared to most of the world. The English word wealth comes from a word meaning well-being. Everything on earth comes from the God who created it, including "the power to get wealth" (Deut.8:18).

As we study these Seven Giving (7G) principles from God's word and put them into practice to manage our finances, they produce a new level of abundance that allows each one of us to become a generous giver in the Kingdom of God. God's principles always begin with a foundation (Mt. 7:24), and the wise and proper handling of our wealth is no exception.

Don't be discouraged today if you find yourself in financial chaos - God has a sure way out (1 Cor. 10:15), and more importantly, God has a way that will bring about true and lasting success to your finances (Josh. 1:8). If you already have a balanced and healthy financial situation, these principles will only serve to increase your ability to maximize and use the resources that you have in your care (Lk 6:38).

Attitude

> "Attitude is a little thing that makes a big difference."
> -- Winston Churchill

Our attitude towards finances develops over many years and from many different influences. We may be careless, selfish, frugal, indifferent, or simply unaware of the profound impact on us, our families, friends, and acquaintances because of the way we think and act regarding money. More marriages end in divorce, more inheritances are legally contested, and more friendships are severed over disagreements about money than for any other reason. Truly, the Bible says it right, "the love of money is a root of all kinds of evil" (1 Tim. 6: 10, NIV). Central to this Bible truth is a person's *attitude* towards money. Our attitude towards money will determine how we will work for, spend, save, and give it away throughout our lifetime.

The Bible has a great deal of wisdom and counsel concerning the handling of personal and collective finances. However, it is truly our attitude that determines our capacity to receive this advice (for example, see Luke 16:9-12, Matthew 6:24, Ecclesiastes 5: 10-15). Market researchers understand the power of attitudes and, therefore, try to shape or influence them to create desire and loyalty for their particular products. The attitude of a Believer, however, must be shaped and strengthened by the word of God (Rom. 12:2, Eph. 3:16).

The attitude of blessing comes through:

- Genuine humility
- Reverence for God and His Word
- Willingness to change negative patterns or lifestyle

Attitude is seated in the mind, and God's word instructs Believers to "have the same mindset as Christ Jesus" (Phil. 2:5, NIV). Jesus had the attitude of a servant who chose to obey his Father's commands at all times (John 8:29); we should, therefore, do likewise.

Attitude is the first principle because everything else is built upon the mindset that we choose, and yes, it is a choice. The Amplified Bible expresses Philippians 2:5 like this:

Let this same attitude and purpose and [humble} mind be in you which was in Christ Jesus: [Let Him be your example in humility:}

Once our mind is made up, once we acknowledge God's word as *the authority* in our life, including how we handle our finances, then all of the wisdom of God can fall into place to bring great blessings to ourselves and to those in need around us.

Attitudes are formed and held in our minds. The attitudes we hold become our "lenses" that we see the world through. Attitudes vary considerably among people concerning:

- Care for the poor and needy
- Giving one-tenth or a "tithe" of our income
- Borrowing or debt
- Saving for retirement or future events

A Godly attitude is the greatest asset in any believer's portfolio because it literally opens the door to every miraculous blessing and provision available. (Prov. 15:33, Mal. 3:8)

Priorities

"But seek first his kingdom and his righteousness, and all these
things will be added to you."
-- Matthew 6:33 (NAS)

The priorities we make in life determine the course of our actions. Consider the ancient story of Cain and Able, the first sons of Adam. Both of them worked and produced something: Able was a shepherd, and Cain was a farmer (Gen. 4:2). The Bible records the different priorities of each man towards God in the next two verses:

And at the end of days, it happened that Cain brought an offering to Jehovah from the fruit of the ground. And Abel brought, he also, from the firstlings of his flocks, even from their fat. And Jehovah looked to Abel and to his offering. (Gen. 4:3-4, GLT)

In her book, Faith Principles in Action: A Study of Foundational Truths, Pastor Janet Kreis presented this concept of the differing priorities of these two brothers (Kreis, 1984). God explicitly approves of Abel's offering but confronts Cain with sin (Gen. 4:6-7). Why? The account shows two different priorities: Cain brought leftovers to God only when it was convenient for him, while Able made it a priority to offer his best first. In Cain's resulting jealousy and anger, he murders his brother Abel (Gen. 4:8). His wrong priorities set him up for failure, grief, and guilt.

Our priorities in life must come from God's word in order to be successful (Mt. 6:33, Prov. 21: 17, 28:20, Lk. 12:21) - there are no exceptions for how we handle our finances. Financial priorities are most clearly demonstrated when we follow a budget. A budget sets priorities before money is ever received or spent. Once we set our priorities, we can measure our progress by comparing what actually happens with the goals we have set up ahead of time. We will explore budgeting in detail in the next lesson on Diligence.

Once we know how to prioritize, it is important (really, crucial) that we actually follow through with a plan. In writing about Leadership, Billy Hornsby wrote this about practicing your priorities (which is really what budgeting is all about):

No matter what you say, what you do speaks volumes more to the people with whom you work. We need to build our values by living out our ideals as much as possible. Then, others will take us seriously when we begin to lead them. (Hornsby, 2005)

Do you still think that you are not influencing anyone by how you handle your personal finances? Think again. Financial stewardship, which is life-giving, is founded upon God's principles. There is no success with a "half-plan."

True success in managing your finances will only come when you set Godly priorities in a measurable plan (Lk. 14:28).

In a practical sense, no discussion about Godly priorities can be complete without addressing the topic of *Tithes* (Lev. 27:30). Christians hold a considerable variety of opinions on the practice of giving a tithe, or *one-tenth,* of income that is dedicated to sacred use. Understanding what the Tithe really represents is essential to the highest and best financial stewardship. When believers approach the idea of tithing with a solid conviction based on the truth of God's word, the results are priorities that lead to successful stewardship.

The tithe is not merely an Old Testament Law of Moses required to support the Levite priests, but rather, it reveals the principle of priorities found throughout the entire Bible. Many examples from the scriptures support this idea of a "tithe principle" (Kreis, 1984, p. 96), or things that have been dedicated or set apart for and to God. These examples stretch back to the tree of knowledge in Eden, pass through the offerings of the law in Israel, and reach beyond the abundant provision of apostolic ministry in the New Testament (Gen. 2:6-7, 2 Chron. 31: 10, Acts 4:35).

A notable example from the Bible of someone who had a spiritual understanding of the tithe was Abraham. Consider the following passages:

And blessed, praised, and glorified be God Most High, Who has given your foes into your hand! And [Abram} gave him a tenth of all he had taken... But Abram said to the king of sodom, I have lifted up my hand and sworn to the Lord, God Most High, the Possessor and Maker of heaven and earth (Gen. 14: 20, 22, AMP.)

Abraham raised his hand to heaven and acknowledged God as his top priority! Immediately after this event, God gives Abraham a vision and tells him, "I am your shield, your very great reward" (Gen. 15: 1, NIV). Abraham recognized God as the "possessor" and "maker" of all by dedicating the tenth and giving these *tithes* to a priest named Melchizedek before the priesthood or tithing was established. Much could be said of the life of Abraham and how his priorities set the course of action that allowed God to abundantly bless him with "riches, honor, and life" (Prov. 22:4, NIV). The tithe is one of the most practical evidences that a believer has made God the most important priority in life.

Diligence

"Energy and Persistence Conquers All Things"
-- Benjamin Franklin

When you combine the rich truth of God's principles with diligence and perseverance, there is nothing in this world that can stop you from accomplishing great things (Jer. 32: 19, 33:3). Diligence can be "tough stuff" it requires commitment and determination. Dave Ramsey refers to this mindset as someone who is "gazelle intense" (Ramsey, 2013). The rewards of diligence, however, are very great.

Before exploring the principle of diligence in finances, let's look at a definition of this word:

Diligence: 1. Constant and earnest effort to accomplish what is undertaken; persistent exertion of body or mind. 2. Law. The degree of care and caution required by the circumstances of a person (Dictionary.com, 2013)

The origin of this word literally has the meaning to choose or to value highly in love (Online Etymology, 2010). When we love God, we demonstrate this by highly valuing his word and by diligently applying his principles to every aspect of our lives. We make the choice to govern our finances according to God's plan and principles. As identified in the previous lesson, a budget is what establishes our financial priorities, and when diligence is applied, it makes their execution a success.

A great example of someone who was diligent in budgeting from the Bible is the story of Joseph (Gen. 41). Joseph had received wisdom from God about a future fourteen-year period that was to be divided between plenty and famine (Gen. 41:25-27). By prioritizing a relatively small amount (one-fifth, or 20 percent) of what was produced, Joseph was able to amass a store during the first seven years that not only lasted during the seven-year famine that followed (Gen. 41:47-54) but enabled Joseph to supply all the other nations with food (Gen. 41:57).

Finances and Budgeting can often seem complex and "fuzzy," but they can be distilled into simpler and more effective terms when we set priorities and follow a basic plan. We have already covered the importance of attitude towards money, and now establishing a basic plan will ensure that we can diligently follow through with our priorities. Joseph had a God-given plan to save 20 percent each year, which he followed and was, therefore, very successful. According to Matthew 6:33, God's plan for our finances prioritizes the kingdom (i.e., the spiritual) and "righteousness" (i.e., doing what is right) and therefore is followed by a supernatural provision of all we need. There is an incredible supernatural aspect to our finances that will be explored later in the lesson on the principle of Faith, but in the next lesson, we first need to discuss the principle that proves everything - Accountability!

In the eBook appendix to this course, there are budget forms with illustrative examples that can be used for any household to establish a "Believer's Budget" to prioritize spending and saving successfully. These forms are tools that have been developed and successfully put into practice by seeking the Godly wisdom of Christian writers and teachers, including Dave Ramsey, the late Larry Burkett, and others. With some diligence, any reader can search out and apply the truth of these principles to their financial stewardship.

Accountability

In this case, moreover, it is required of stewards that one be found
trustworthy.
-- 1 Corinthians 4:2 (NAS)

Stewardship is most closely related to the idea of accountability - being willing and able to give an account of your actions, especially your financial actions. Stewardship was the first test given to the human race in the garden of Eden, and it was the first failure when Adam and Eve tried to hide their actions from God and avoid responsibility for being held trustworthy. (Gen. 3:8)

Accountability always leads back to God and his word. We cannot avoid the truth of God's requirement and our obligation to remain accountable. Mankind's failure at stewardship from the beginning reveals our true dependence on God. Consider the following roles:

- God is the creator and "owner" of everything, seen and unseen
- People are "stewards" or caretakers over the earth
- Satan is the "tempter" who intends to deceive and destroy

These three roles are important in understanding successful financial stewardship because they reveal the principle of accountability in terms that do not change with time. As creator and owner of everything, we honor God as our source (Prov. 3:9), we exercise due care over the things entrusted to us by virtue of our delegated stewardship, and God's word holds the authority over the tempter who comes to "rob, kill, and destroy" (Jn. 10: 10) anything of value that we have.

In order for a steward to remain trustworthy and accountable, there must be a plan in place. In the previous lesson, we discussed the application of diligence to a budget or financial plan. If you have no written budget to plan how to spend your money, you are easily on your way to failure, otherwise known as average. You cannot excel without a plan. God prepares plans (Jer. 29: 11), and we should follow his example in our finances.

One way of planning monthly expenses uses an Allocated Spending Plan (ramseysolutions.com/budgeting/useful-forms) or an *Assigned* Spending Plan that I have modified to look something like the following (note the numerical order for priority):

Assigned Monthly Spending Plan

Description	%	Amount	Balance
Earnings - monthly	100%	$3,000	$3,000
Expenses:			
1. Tithes	10%	300	2,700
2. Savings	5%	150	2,550
3. Housing	32%	960	1,590
4. Utilities	8%	240	1,350
5. Food & Supplies	11%	330	1,020
6. Transportation	14%	420	600
7. Medical/Health	4%	120	480
8. Clothing	3%	90	390
9. Personal	4%	120	270
10. Charity	3%	90	180
11. Recreation	3%	90	90
12. Debt	3%	90	0
Balance			$0

The spending plan assigns each dollar of expected income to designated categories and amounts of expense in a relatively prioritized order from highest to lowest and then tracks the remaining balance until everything is assigned. Try not to get overly concerned with specific percentages or categories. Budgeting is about accountability, and this should be done in terms that most people can understand. There are really only two basic percentages that you must remember and budget for in your plan: 10% is the tithe that belongs to God, and 100% is the maximum percentage of your income that you should be spending. A plan accomplishes a number of critically important goals: First and foremost, it honors God with the tithe. Like Abel, we honor God first by offering a holy portion before any other consideration of expense. Like Abraham, we recognize God with our tithes as the creator and maker of all things and simultaneously, we acknowledge our position as steward over the things he has provided for us. This approach also prioritizes the remainder of our spending by identifying those things or expenses that are most necessary beginning with a systematic plan for saving. Next, we prioritize our most necessary living expenses, such as housing and related costs, food, etc. By assigning out how we plan to spend all of our anticipated income, we will have the tools to form a budget and will avoid the tendency toward "splurge" spending. Some will look at this plan and say, "I can't make it work; I don't have enough to meet my bills," but remember, the point of this exercise is to get a written plan and then diligently begin leaving the miracles to God!

The forms in the appendix expand on these categories of monthly expenses so that at the beginning of each month, you can enter the details on a worksheet that makes up each of the 12 categories. You are able to modify the categories and the percentages to meet your individual plan. The budget forms will also allow for additional types of income or deposits to keep your monthly tracking in agreement with your bank and other records.

One of the most important areas of accountability concerns debt. We have all found ourselves in debt at some time in life. In fact, Christ paid our debt at the cross because we were spiritually bankrupt and could never redeem ourselves. There is no question that debt brings bondage and robs us of income that we could choose to use in some other way (hopefully to help others with their needs). Debt repayments on a monthly basis will also rob your other budget categories and interfere with your goal of prioritizing your spending. Recognizing that most people have debt simply emphasizes the importance of having a written plan to move in the opposite direction toward debt-free living.

A very effective tool to do this is what Dave Ramsey refers to as the "Debt Snowball." The concept is really a debt *repayment* snowball, and you begin by making a list of all of your debts from smallest to largest (if you own a home, your mortgage can be excluded from this exercise in the short term). You continue to make monthly payments while diligently concentrating on paying off the first debt, and then as each debt is paid off entirely you assign the old payment to the next larger debt so that your repayments "snowball" and each debt is reduced as quickly as possible. The following charts illustrate the Debt Snowball process (based on the author's actual debt snowball experience many years ago) notice in just four months and a modest income that a whopping $10,799 in debt was paid off!

Debt Snowball (actual experience of author):

Started January

22, 2013

Account	Start_debt	Min_pymt	New_pymt	Balance	No.
Install. Card #1	$350	$25	$25	$350	24
Bank loan #1	1900	89	114	1900	36
Install. Card #2	3300	121	235	3,300	36
Auto loan #1	4737	433	668	4,737	28
Auto loan #2	5212	179	847	5,212	24
Totals	$15,499			$15,499	

DEBT REDUCTION TO-DATE: (10,799)

Debt Snowball

Progress date: May 22, 2013

Account	Start_debt	Min_pymt	New_pymt	Balance	No.
Install. Card #1	$350	$25	$25	$0	
Bank loan #1	1900	89	114	0	
Install. Card #2	3300	121	235	0	
Auto loan #1	4737	433	668	0	
Auto loan #2	5212	179	847	4,700	20
Totals	$15,499			$4,700	

Don't be overly concerned with interest rates or exact balances - simply list debts from smallest to largest and proceed. When a debt is paid off, the prior payment is added to the next debt. The minimum payment for credit cards should not be the company's required minimum payment, if at all possible, given your own budget constraints. You should set this minimum at the 3-year payoff shown on your statement or higher and work from there. The results of this process will give the borrower needed encouragement and build momentum to pay off remaining future debt balances. The balance owed and number of payments can be quickly inserted on the snowball schedule at anytime from a monthly statement, but the starting debt amounts are left on the worksheet to allow another encouraging calculation: total debt reduction to date! The debt snowball is purposely not linked to the spending plan or budget to allow for a quick and easy update at any time to get a picture of where the debt situation stands. This tool will help to keep you accountable for living within your means (remember the 100%) and show progress toward debt-free living. One important note to keep in mind: the spending plan is the standard guide under normal circumstances, but the debt-snowball requires an all-out attack on your debt, including birthday gifts and tax refunds, etc, using any and all available resources toward reducing those balances owed.

Faith

Now faith is the substance of things hoped for, the evidence of things
not seen.
-- Hebrews 11: 1 (KJV)

Faith is a spiritual principle that functions in a world of substance
and evidence. How we handle our finances in this world often reveals
what our real faith values are about the world to come. But God is so
faithful that when we give honor to him, he also honors us in return
through the invisible working of faith.

In economics, an influential early father named Adam Smith wrote
a book titled *The Wealth of Nations*. This book, written in the same
year as America's declaration of independence, "sought to reveal the
nature and cause of a nation's prosperity" (www.econlib.org). Smith
goes on to historically write of a metaphorical "invisible hand" that
operates within every economy to promote the production of greater
value than any individual intended on his own. Faith operates in the
same manner as this invisible hand, often unseen and unexplainable,
yet always present with the believer to provide all sufficiency (2 Cor.
9:8) in every circumstance, according to his power that works in us
(Eph. 3:20-21). Faith does not always make sense, but it always
prevails.

Financial stewardship for believers cannot be separated from faith.
Faith makes it all possible. Faith will produce a surplus when the
natural understanding only sees a deficit. If you are not relying on God
to make a supernatural provision for you, then unfortunately, you will
not be successful, and these principles will not work for you. On the
other hand, if you are fully trusting that God is able to make all grace
abound to you and give you a sufficiency of all you need, then it does
not matter what your income level or occupation is -God's promises
are for all who believe, and he doesn't respect one person over another
(Acts 10:34).

Like the grain of mustard seed that Jesus spoke about (Mt. 17:20, Lk. 17:6), your faith will multiply your finances until every need is met and you have an abundance to help others. Only what is done through faith will endure (Mt. 24: 13, 1 John 5:4). Only faith pleases God (Heb. 11:6), and therefore, faith must be central to our financial stewardship if we want to please God in this crucial area of our life. Faith takes little and feeds many, raises dead situations to life, and gives us complete victory no matter how hopeless a situation may appear. Faith is taken in small steps: Honor God by Tithing. Do what is right (your best effort). Expect miracles to happen.

Faith is protective, a shield against the enemy (Eph. 6: 16) that would rob us and decimate our finances (Jn.10: 10). But faith is also proactive, a step out of the boat (Mt. 14:29) to walk on complete uncertainty. Many times, people are sincerely afraid to take a walk of faith, especially in the area of finances. Jesus, however, remains close by to offer a strong hand of guidance and encouragement. Faith is not complicated but simple and sincere. If you have the faith to honor God with 10%, he will prove his power to provide 100% - in any situation, for anyone who believes.

Generosity

In everything I did, I showed you that by this kind of hard work, we must help the weak, remembering the words the Lord Jesus himself said: 'It is more blessed to give than to receive.'
-- Acts 20:35 (NIV)

Generosity is awesome! Think about those times in your life when you were in need, really in need, and someone came along and just poured out generosity to you. And even though you may have appreciated it at the time, think about what that person experienced. They experienced being generous, willing, and able to help someone in need, and they reached beyond themselves the same way that God acts towards us all the time.

In the next lesson, we will expand the discussion on joy, but for now, it is important to understand that joy and love for others motivate us to be generous. Generosity is not, and cannot be, a legal requirement for believers. It must come from the heart, not a religious formula.

The simple truth about generosity is that you have to first have something to share in order to be generous. In financial stewardship, we honor God with our substance and the first fruits of our increase (Prov. 3:9). God gives us increase and the power to obtain wealth (Deut. 8: 18) so that we become good stewards of those material things.

God promises to make us a blessed people, the seed of Abraham, who lend to many nations and are not borrowers (Deut. 15:6, 28: 12). All of these references prove that God intends for us to be faithful stewards (1 Cor. 4:2) that have resources to generously supply to those in need. Now for the reality check: many of us are broke and in debt, with nothing to give to the needs of others, let alone honor God with our substance and tithes. What went wrong? If you guessed there is a thief in this story, you are correct! The same liar and embezzler that stole mankind's stewardship over paradise in the beginning is still at work in our generation. If we will be a generous people, we must have a change of attitude and priorities, followed by a diligent and accountable pursuit of God and his principles, before we can obtain through faith our spiritual and financial heritage.

Joy

The people rejoiced over the offerings, for they had given freely and wholeheartedly to the LORD, and King David was filled with joy.

-- 1 Chronicles 29:9 (NLT)

Joy is an exhilarating human emotion that transcends happiness or anything like it. Jesus himself was motivated to go to the cross because of joy (Heb. 12:2). It is one of the few emotions experienced both in heaven and on earth (Job 38:7, Psa. 5:11). It reaches its fullest expression in the presence of God (Psa. 16:11). Joy is worth living for and dying for because it is one of the supernatural rewards that results from giving to others (Psa. 35:27). Joy also has a prolific nature - when we give others joy, we receive more joy back because joy multiplies itself (Lk. 6:38).

John D. Rockefeller was a tithe-paying philanthropist who gave money away for the sheer joy of it (www.wealthymatters.com). Yet today, Rockefeller's name is most remembered because of the vast wealth he accumulated. In today's dollars, adjusted for inflation, Rockefeller likely accumulated over $189.6 Billion dollars and gave away an estimated $550 million dollars during his 98-year lifespan (www.wikipedia.org), making him perhaps the richest man in history!

God's word has much to say about wealth, for it is God who gives us the power to get wealth (Deut. 8: 18). Throughout the Bible, faithful financial stewardship is associated with people who were joyful givers (Abraham, Joseph, David, Zaccheus, and Jesus - to name a few). Joyful financial stewardship comes through and is associated with the following:

— Obedience to God's word and principles
— Miraculous provision
— Abundance
— Generosity

In one of Jesus' most enigmatic sayings, "It is more blessed (Gk. "Makarios") to give than to receive," he reveals the great joy and well-being that comes from giving to others. Biblical stewardship illuminates the path that actualizes this ability to give to others in need while providing the intrinsic reward of joy to the giver. Effective and fulfilling stewardship will always result from a return to these proven foundational principles

Notes

Franklin, Benjamin (1748) Advice to a Young Tradesman. Retrieved from http://www.angelfire.com/biz3/eserve/ayt.html

Hornsby, Billy (2005) Success for the Second in Command: Practice what you say you value -your priorities

Kreis, Janet E. (1984) FAITH PRINCIPLES IN ACTION: A Study of Foundational Truths

Ramsey, Dave https://www.ramseysolutions.com

Smith, Adam (1776) The Wealth of Nations. The concise encyclopedia of economics. http://www.econlib.org

King Solomon (1,000 B.C.), Chapter 2, verse 15 (NIV) Retrieved from http://bible.cc/songs/2-15.htm

Churchill, Winston (xxxx),http://www career-success-for-newbies.com/attitude-quotes.html

DaVinci, Leonardo (xxxx), http://www .goodreads.com/quotes/tag/attitude

diligence. (n.d.). Dictionary.com Unabridged. Retrieved from Dictionary.com website: http://dictionary.reference.com/browse/diligence

Bible version quotations:

New International Version (NIV)

Amplified Version (AMP)

New American Standard Version (NAS)

King James Version (KJV)

New Living Translation (NLT)

Cover design by Amanda Lewis

Electronic forms for the Believer's Budget are available as a link in the appendix to the eBook version of Seven Giving Principles for Biblical Financial Success.

For more information about this book, contact the author: Greg Wright, Mountain City, TN 37683 gwpreach1@gmail.com

Greg Wright is the former Executive Director of Finance at Bayside Community Church in Bradenton, Florida and has been licensed as a CPA for many years. Greg was ordained as a minister of the gospel in 2002 by Dr. David J. Minor, Coudersport Gospel Tabernacle, Coudersport, Pennsylvania. Greg has a Bachelor of Science in Accounting degree from Penn State University, State College, Pennsylvania, and in 2012, he received his master's degree in public policy and administration from Northwestern University in Evanston, Illinois, however, he credits all of his success to the Lord Jesus Christ, including the revealed principles in this book.

Greg is married to Pamela Rae Snyder Wright and lives in Mountain City Tennessee. You may contact the author at: gwpreach1@gmail.com

www.ingramcontent.com/pod-product-compliance
Lightning Source LLC
Chambersburg PA
CBHW071300130726
47998CB00003B/1273